*"Of all the places
I've been I love
Tasmania the most"*

For the
LOVE
of
TASMANIA

Port Arthur at sunrise.

For the LOVE of TASMANIA

Photographs by OWEN HUGHES
Text by MARTIN GILMOUR

'GREEN GABLES'

PUBLISHED & DISTRIBUTED BY OWEN HUGHES
17 Elizabeth Street, Launceston, Tasmania 7250. Australia, Telephone: (003) 31 1481.

Reprinted 1987.
First Published 1985 First Printing.
© Copyright 1985: Owen Hughes and Martin Gilmour.
All right reserved. Designed by Owen Hughes and Martin Gilmour.
Colour separations, printing & binding by Dai Nippon Printing Co., Ltd. in Japan.
Typeset by Duo Typesetting, 44 Connaught Crescent, Launceston, Tasmania 7250. Australia.
© Copyright Map of Tasmania: Mercury-Walch Printers, Moonah 7000. Hobart, Tasmania, Australia.
National Library of Australia Card Number and ISBN 0-9590145-0-0

Copies of most of these pictures are available in large sizes suitable for home
or office decor.

FOREWORD

By Sir Raymond Ferrall C.B.E.

The classic examples of photographic art in this finely produced work by Tasmania's Owen Hughes are all of his own choice. Yet, as such I believe they would be a true reflection of a wide variety of many other knowledgeable and aesthetic tastes.

Unlike so many other art forms, the camera records just what it sees. It falls then to the skilled eye behind the lens to use vast and experienced talents to produce a composition inhibited with the mood of the occasion, the place, and the subject. Though it be a rather platitudinous example, there would be an underlying vein of sentiment, love, and deep affection in the picture of a young couple on their wedding day. Likewise, the study of towering mountains and great gorges must reflect a sense of majesty, while a gently flowing stream meandering placidly through its green surrounding meadows would record peace and tranquility.

It is in these that the finesse and mastery of Owen Hughes is so vividly portrayed.

But, of course there is so much more to it. So many of today's photographers have neither the technical skills, versatility, nor inclination - probably for a variety of good reasons - to complete their artistry in the very considerable dark room part. It is there that the photographer's testing time lies, for he must be nothing if not a perfectionist, endowed with immense patience, and above all a sense of imagination that will prompt him to maintain in his work the very same moods that were with him when he shot the picture.

I need scarcely add that Owen Hughes is one of that rare race of artists who carry out the highly involved photographic processes in their entirety. His work, in fact, is a splendid amalgam of inspiration followed by great technical skills. These are the simple reasons which have won him national acclaim and gained him the prized accolade of Master of Photography by the prestigious Institute of Australian Photography.

"For The Love of Tasmania" is his own title for this broad selection of his most eminent work. The pictures within are a true reflection of the artistry of Owen Hughes and possess a deep enchanting beauty.

Longford dawn.

ACKNOWLEDGEMENTS

Photography to me is a means of conveying the beauty and mood of a particular scene or place.

It is often the cold winter morning which is the most beautiful, not because I like the cold, but because the fog isolates sections and creates simplicity in the beauty of a particular subject.

I would like to take this opportunity to thank those closest to me for encouragement they have shown in the concept and production of this book.

Marcia for her patience, understanding and encouragement during long hours of work and planning.

My three daughters, Anita, Shelly and Jeanette, for their input of young ideas.

Malcolm Lord for the fastidious attention shown in the processing of transparencies.

Peter Hay for the early morning plane flights in his Cessna 172 to obtain the aerial photographs.

Sir Raymond Ferrall for the kind words in his foreword.

Lesley, my receptionist, for the extra work load placed upon her.

Martin Gilmour for his enthusiasm in the production and design.

Bob Green for the use of his photograph of the Tasmanian Tiger.

To all those people who participated in the book and to all my customers who, without their patronage over many years, For The Love of Tasmania would not have been possible.

Thank You

Owen Hughes

OWEN HUGHES

CONTENTS

First light on Ben Lomond.

Previous page: Patchwork meadows near Devonport.

INTRODUCTION

A wild stretch of water 240km wide called Bass Strait separates Tasmania from mainland Australia - it also protects a way of life jealously guarded by many people.

Tasmania is more than an island with ragged peaks, wild rivers, chalk white beaches and rolling pastureland.

It represents a rare quality of life. Smog is unheard of, children grow up with values and opportunities are limited only by an individual's imagination.

As quality of life becomes an ever-pressing goal for many people, so the diverse attraction offered by Tasmania becomes more attractive.

There is a wonderland of natural beauty with more than 96 national parks and reserves occupying nearly 10 per cent of the State.

The rich convict background, where thousands of men and women were transported, many for trivial crimes, is intrinsically woven into everyday life.

The stark beauty of early colonisation pitted against the harsh and unyielding elements is preserved for all to remember.

Port Arthur and the Isle of the Dead, Port Macquarie and the ring of mountains which forced escaped convicts to canabalism in their quest for freedom - it all remains.

Tasmania is legitimately called the most English of all Australian States.

The orchards, hawthorn hedges and hopfields; the wild lake country; the early freestone architecture and the roadside villages dotted with elms, oaks and poplars.

But more prevalent is the stunning array of natural beauty.

The likes of Cradle Mountain with its untamed and often deadly beauty; the highland tarns of which many are still un-named and the rugged South-West wilderness with rivers powerful enough to carve gorges through mountains and turn the tide of governments.

It is no surprise that Tasmania has become a paradise for tourists.

Within an hour by car from any part of the island the terrain can change from deserted beaches, to pastureland, rain forests and eventually wilderness.

Just as close is a first class hotel or the sophistication of casinos and dancing girls.

Tasmania is not perfect, but it is blessed with a special touch of old world magic.

Coles Bay is one of the most popular holiday resorts on Tasmania's East Coast. Sheltered by the Freycinet Peninsula, Coles Bay is a particularly good boating area.

The Tamar River paddle-steamer Lady Stelfox beneath Ritchies Art Mill on the Tamar River.
The Lady Stelfox was built by the owner of the Penny Royal World, Mr. Roger Smith.

13

The magnificent sight of Wineglass Bay which greets walkers in the Freycinet National Park, at Coles Bay, on Tasmania's East Coast.

An aerial view of Bicheno. On the left is the tip of Diamond Island and the major beach on the right is Red Bill Beach.

The popular pastime of fishing off wharves. Here Joe and Tom try their luck off the Stanley Wharf.

Opposite page: Mr. A. J. Nicholson, of Table Cape, with the beautiful view from his property. Poppies are growing in the field behind.

Trout fishing author Don Gilmour stalking a fish in the shallows at Little Pine Lagoon in the Central Highlands. Little Pine Lagoon is world renowned for its outstanding fly-fishing sport.

An aerial shot of Hobart City. The central business district is in the background with the wharf area, Salamanca Place and the original seamen's quarters at Battery Point in the foreground.

The Grange homestead at Campbell Town in the Midlands, 68km south of Launceston.
The Grange is used extensively for Adult Education classes.

The snow-capped peaks of the Frankland Ranges in the South-West with Lake Pedder beneath the mist in the background.

The Nabowla Lavender Farm 54km from Launceston. The lavender oil is in great demand by other countries and during the picking season it is a popular destination for tourists.

The headwaters of the Mersey River as it winds through ferns and beech trees.

Next page: Mustering cattle on Jack and Joan Bellinger's property, McRaes Hills near Cressy. Dry's Bluff, a peak of the Western Tiers is in the background.

23

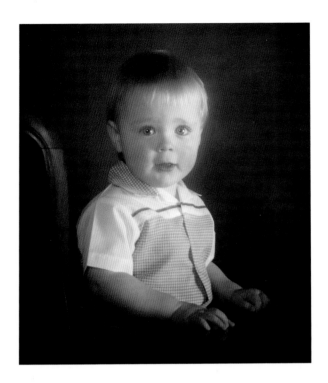

Alexis Hayes.

Luke Bennetts.

Jeff and Yvonne O'Byrne, of Launceston, and their family.

Rosie Behlau who was the Tasmanian Mannequin of the Year 1984-85.

The Private Collection

"Taken at 8.00 a.m. on a winter's morning from the Tamar Rowing Club pontoon at Launceston. F5.6 at 1/125 second with a 150mm lens and Vericolor commercial film. The ghost-like effect is created naturally by the fog blocking out the blackground."

Huon Mystic

"Taken at 4.30 p.m. on a winter's afternoon on the Huon River. F4 at 1/15 second with a 300mm lens and Vericolor film."

Huon Solitaire

"A lone yacht on the Huon River at dusk in winter. F4 at 1/30 second with Vericolor commercial film."

Blessington Peace

"Sheep grazing in the mist at Blessington at 10.00 a.m. on a spring morning. F11 at 1/250 second with a 300mm lens and Vericolor film."

Meadow Clouds

"Horses grazing on river flats below Trevallyn, near Launceston. The intriguing cloud-like effect is simply frost and low level mist. F4 at 1/30 second with a 300mm lens and Ektachrome 64 film."

Evening Rays

"Rays of sunlight catch mist forming beneath an oak tree at Entally House. F5.6 at 1/60 second with a 100mm lens and Vericolor film."

Tamar Mist

"The Tamar River moorings with Launceston City in the background. The fog makes the sun appear like the moon. Taken at 7.30 a.m. in August. F8 at 1/250 second with a 100mm lens and Vericolor film."

"Tamar River near Rosevears at 7.30 a.m. in May. Split-second timing was required to catch the seagull flying to its mate sitting on the post. F11 at 1/250 second with a 150mm lens and Vericolor film."

Phantom Fleet

"Fishing boats at St. Helens shortly after sunrise. Mist rising off the water gives a phantom-like effect.
F11 at 1/125 second with a 100mm lens and Ektachrome 64 film."

Little Liffey Falls

"Taken near the Liffey Falls during heavy rain. The slow shutter speed creates the creamy effect on the water. F22 at 1/2 second with 100mm lens and Vericolor commercial film."

Moon In Blue

"Peron Sands at St. Helens with the last evening light. F2.8 at 1/4 second with a 150mm lens and Vericolor film."

Evening Sea

"Redbill Beach at Bicheno with Diamond Island in the background. F8 at 1/60 second with a 50mm wide angle lens using Vericolor film."

Misty Moon

"The moon dipping over the Western Tiers at dawn in mid-June. Photograph taken from the Midlands Highway just south of Perth. F4 at 1/60 second with a 300mm lens using Vericolor film."

NORTH
AND NORTH-EAST

Trade has always been the cornerstone of Launceston's development.

Despite being the second largest city in Tasmania, Launceston is the trade and tourism centre of the State.

Bell Bay, close to where the original settlement was made by William Paterson at York Town in 1804, is the major port for the island.

The site for Launceston 60km inland from the mouth of the Tamar River was eventually picked because of its superior agricultural potential.

It quickly became the hub of a thriving farming industry which spread south to the Midlands, west towards Deloraine and north-east toward Scottsdale.

Because of its geographically central position, Launceston is a popular starting and finishing point for tourists.

It is situated at the confluence of the South and North Esk rivers and much further inland than all other major cities.

This results in a continental type climate with about 50 frosty days each year.

Launceston has a vast array of attractions well suited to day trips.

The closest and easily the most popular is the Cataract Gorge and First Basin Reserve.

Situated a few minutes walk from the centre of the city, the Gorge was described this way be settler William Collins in 1804 - "I observed a large fall of water over rocks, nearly a quarter of a mile up a straight gully between perpendicular rocks about 150ft. high. The beauty of the scene is probably not surpassed in the world".

About the turn of this century a walkway was built along the side of the Gorge and a suspension bridge was built across the South Esk at the head of the First Basin.

In 1972 a magnificent chairlift was built across this huge natural basin which incorporates the longest single chairlift span in the world of 308 metres.

Further up the South Esk is the remains of the Duck Reach turbine driven power station. Launceston became the first city south of the Equator to be lit by electricity generated by water power on 10th December, 1895.

The area around Launceston is dotted with many historically classified towns and magnificent Victorian and Georgian mansions.

Places well worthy of visiting include the Batman Bridge, an A-frame bridge across the Tamar River 30km North of Launceston; the historic town of Evandale 19km south of Launceston; the waterfall and lavender farm of Lilydale 27km east of Launceston; the Penny Royal tourist complex in the centre of Launceston and the Federal Country Club Casino.

Tasmania's East Coast offers many kilometres of the most beautiful beaches in Australia.

St. Helens, Bicheno, Swansea and Coles Bay are popular tourist destinations with first class facilities and the attraction of uncluttered beaches.

Mrs. Margaret Carey outside her Cimitiere Street home near Launceston's Glebe area.

The hub of Launceston – the intersection of St. John Street and Brisbane Street taken from the top of the Myer building. On the left is the Launceston Hotel, one of the oldest hotels in Australia, and on the right is the eastern end of the City Mall.

Launceston radio personality Mr. Peter Kaye with the final of the Le Specs Action Girl competition in the Quadrant Mall.

Right: The mixture of looks of concern, delight and anticipation as the field of the 1985 Launceston Cup enter the home straight at Mowbray Racecourse.

Above: Launceston's First Basin packed with thousands of people for the annual summer rock concert. The First Basin is a spectacular natural feature only a few minutes drive from the centre of Launceston. In the background is the suspension bridge built in 1904.

Launceston's Gorge Bridge during a winter flood. An attractive walkway was built up the right hand side of the Gorge in 1899 and the area is now fully floodlit at night.

Dawn breaks on the city of Launceston. Elizabeth Street looking east.

Susan Wryell with little friend Mark Diprose at Carols by Candlelight in Launceston.

Opposite page: Launceston's principle Catholic Church, the Church of Apostles, in Margaret Street.

Anne and Greg Glass in the City Park.

Opposite page: The rotunda in Launceston's City Park at dawn. The City Park is just a few minutes walk from the central business district.

Corriedale sheep penned after shearing at Bell's property, Sillwood near Carrick, 17km from Launceston.

Shearers during a smoko and in action at a Fingal property. Tasmania is renowned for producing the best superfine wool in the world.

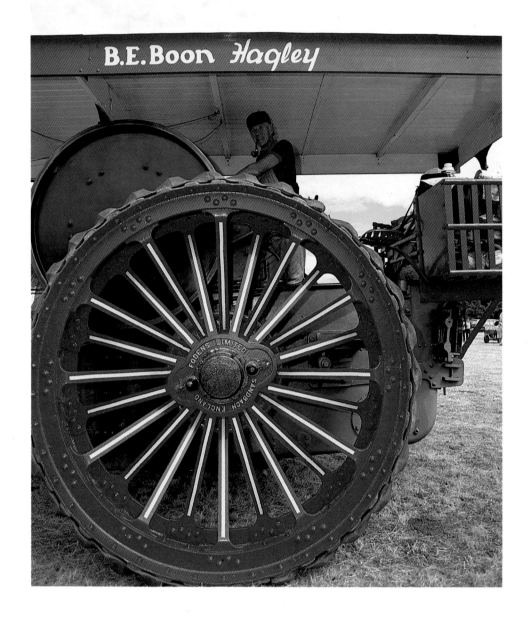

Brian Phair with Bernard Boon's faithfully restored steam engine on display at the Hagley Steam Day.

Previous page: A wide angled aerial shot of the mouth of the Tamar River taken from 3000 metres. George Town and Bell Bay are on the right and Beauty Point on the left.

Above: The peaceful historical village of Evandale, 19km from Launceston, comes to life every year for the annual fair and Australian Pennyfarthing Championships.

Right: East Coast personality Rusty Richards with his bullock team at Goshen just inland from St. Helens.

The mist rises from the South Esk River looking north toward the township of Perth. The South Esk begins its journey in the Fingal Valley and passes through the First Basin and Cataract Gorge to the Tamar River.

The peaceful dawn setting of cattle grazing under gum trees in Tasmania's rural-rich Midlands.

Scottsdale farmer Fred Bissett with his dogs Rusty and Biddy. Scottsale is one of the richest agricultural and forestry areas situated 63km north-east of Launceston.

Peas by the truckload from Steel's property at Winnaleah, near Scottsdale. Tasmania is the major producer of frozen vegetables in Australia.

Left: B. and L. Breadmore's store in the North-East Coast resort town of Bridport.

Below: The main beach at Bridport.

Opposite page: Tasmanian Photographic Model of the Year Bronwyn Sellers at Bridport Beach.

Left: Pyengana axeman Eric Rattray in action at the Fingal Coal Festival.

Below: Len Coker pours a beer at the Weldborough pub for locals Harry and Faye Musicka.

North-East identity Max Krushka in his garden at Derby. Derby was an important tin mining town in the late 1800s and a Mine Museum has recorded the area's history.

Left: Popular surf fishing beach Swimcart near St. Helens, with Binnalong Bay in the background.

Right: Bicheno crayfisherman Leon Cruse sets pots at dawn, from Kerry Semmen's boat. Bicheno is one of the State's major fishing ports on the East Coast and is 174km from Launceston and 195km from Hobart.

Below: An aerial shot of resort town Scamander with St. Patrick's Head and Elephant Pass in the background.

Left: My family friends Ron and Doreen Lohrey in their garden at St. Marys. Ron was the butcher at St. Marys for many years.

Below: St. Patricks Head in the Fingal Valley near St. Marys.

My brother Brian in his magnificent flower garden at Bicheno. Brian is a farmer and local identity.

Next page: Ben Lomond shrouded in a magnificent crimson sunset pictured from the Fingal Valley.

The rural setting of Whitemark on Flinders Island with Mt. Strezlecki in the background.

The Flinders Island fishing port of Lady Barron with the golden tips of sunrise.

SOUTH

Nestled beneath the grandeur of Mt. Wellington is Tasmania's capital city Hobart, one of the most attractive capitals in Australia.

It is a city based upon its life link, the Derwent River.

Australia's blue water yachting classic the Sydney to Hobart race ends in the Derwent River and nearly half the city's employees commute across the river to work.

Few people realise Hobart is Australia's second oldest city, being founded in 1804 by John Bowen.

A settlement was originally made in southern Tasmania for strategic reasons after Governor King heard rumours that the French planned to settle there.

The first settlement on the Derwent River was made at Risdon, up stream from the eventual site chosen the next year by David Collins.

Historically Hobart and Southern Tasmania is a gold mine.

Salamanca Place on the waterfront boasts Georgian warehouses dating back to the whaling days of the 1830s which are occupied today by restaurants, art galleries, craft shops and taverns. Every Saturday morning the area springs to life with the famous Salamanca Market.

A short distance from Salamanca Place is Battery Point, the original quarters for the seamen of Hobart Town.

The area is unspoilt with quaint cottages flanking narrow lanes and village greens.

Hobart has more than 90 buildings classified by the National Trust including Australia's oldest theatre the Theatre Royal built in 1837.

Hobart is well known for Wrest Point Casino which was Australia's first licensed casino.

There are many fascinating attractions in and around Hobart.

Most visitors to Southern Tasmania rarely leave without seeing Port Arthur and the settlement of Richmond.

Port Arthur is about 100km from Hobart on the Tasman Peninsular.

This area of Tasmania is infamous for the penal settlement between 1830 and 1877.

It was ideal for this purpose with only a narrow isthmus known as Eaglehawk Neck connecting it to the mainland.

During the days of the penal settlement this was guarded by soldiers and chained hounds.

Few convicts escaped, with Martin Cash being the best known.

Just offshore from Port Arthur is the Isle of the Dead where more than 2000 convicts, free men and soldiers were buried during the life of the settlement.

Richmond argueably has the greatest concentration of historic buildings in a small area and is only 30 minutes drive from Hobart.

About an hour's drive from Hobart is Lake Pedder and Lake Gordon which are equally popular for their trout fishing and breath-taking scenery.

The rotunda during autumn in Hobart's St. David's Park with the city in the background.

Previous page: Dawn breaks over Hobart. The Wrest Point Casino and Convention Centre is in the foreground and behind is the central business district.

Two of Hobart's most famous landmarks – the Tasman Bridge and the towering Mt. Wellington taken from the eastern shore of the Derwent River.

Left: Arthur Circus in Battery Point. The original cottages where Hobart's first sailors lived have been tastefully restored.

Below: Hobart's Salamanca Place which is a popular market on the waterfront every Saturday morning. Mt. Wellington is in the background.

The 60m high Shot Tower at Taroona overlooking the Derwent River. The Shot Tower was built in 1870 and the site is currently an extensive museum and art workshop open to the public.

Hobart is famous as the finishing point of the Sydney to Hobart blue water ocean classic. Above is Victoria Dock, which is primarily used by fishing boats, and on the opposite page is Constitution Dock where the racing yachts are moored.

Two examples of early settlement towns in central Tasmania. Top: The general store at Tunbridge, which is owned by Mrs. Hazelwood and the sleepy hamlet of Ross, a further 14km north. Both towns were vital for changing horses in the days of horse-drawn transport.

Opposite page: The castle-like structure of Hobart's Cascade Brewery through the dappled light of an elm tree. The Cascade Brewery is Australia's oldest, being established in 1824.

Geeveston photographer and close friend Richard Bennett.

*Previous page: The Sentinel Range in the South West wilderness area with Lake Pedder
beneath the clouds.*

The southern orchard areas of Cygnet (right) and Franklin.
Franklin was named after Governor Sir John Franklin and the Huon River is used for the southern schools Head of the River rowing event.

The final wisps of mist still linger in the rich southern rural area of the Arve Valley, near Geeveston.

Opposite page: Mt. La Perouse and the Swallow's Nest Lakes in the South West wilderness. Mt. La Perouse is 1157m high with an unusual sandstone plateau.

Daybreak at Bushy Park in the Derwent Valley.

Mt. Weld emerges from a sea of fiery gold in the rugged South West.

Bathurst Harbour.

Prion Bay in the far south of Tasmania with the New River on the right and the Ironbound Ranges in the background.

Opposite page: The silhouette of Maatsuyker Island which is the home of the southern most lighthouse in Australia.

Kettering off the South-East Coast. A ferry leaves here for popular Bruny Island. The crossing takes about 35 minutes. The native name for the island is Lunawannaalonna.

Right: The neat formality of hopfields near Bushy Park, 56km from Hobart. Hops grown here are used in the brewing of beer.

Below: The upper reaches of the Derwent River near Bushy Park on a still autumn morning.

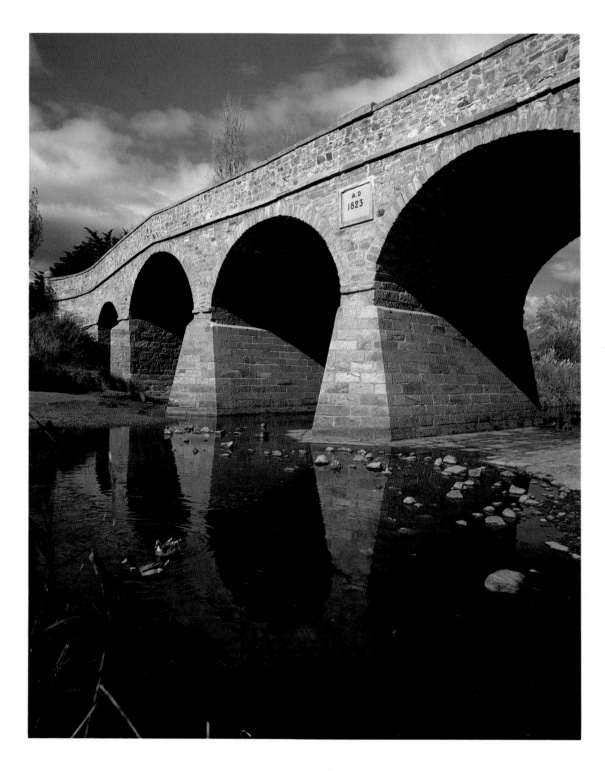

The superb architecture of the Richmond Bridge, 26km from Hobart. The Richmond Bridge is the oldest freestone bridge in Australia being built in 1823.

Two views of Tasmania's No. 1 tourist attraction, Port Arthur. During its 47 years as a penal settlement, Port Arthur earned an infamous reputation. The area abounds with historical sites and many museums and craft shops.

Left: Cape Hauy between Eaglehawk Neck and Tasman Island on Tasmania's South-East Coast.

Below: Tasman Island on the South-East Coast. Cape Pillar, Cape Hauy and Cape Surville are in the background.

Opposite page: The natural phenomenon of tessellated pavement at Eaglehawk Neck.

Cape Raoul and the appropriately named Organ Pipes in the silver-grey light of dawn.

Previous page: The rugged, yet peaceful setting of Pirates Bay with the Tasman Peninsula stretching into the distance.

Top: Morris' General Store at Swansea. Built of stone it is a good example of early colonial architecture.

Above: The settlement on Maria Island National Park. This is a popular island for bushwalkers and fishing boat transport to the island is available from Triabunna.

NORTH-WEST
and WEST

Primary industry has made Tasmania's North-West and West Coast part of the State's richest areas.

Fertile land for agriculture and grazing, massive forests and the mineral and fishing wealth of the West Coast.

Inland there is a unique treasure in the Cradle Mountain and Lake St. Clair National Park.

Nearly 4000 people walk the Cradle Mountain Overlander Track each year and it is clearly the State's premier national park.

The two principle areas of population along the North-West Coast are Devonport and Burnie.

Devonport is sited at the mouth of the Mersey River and officially became a town in 1890 with the merging of the west bank township of Formby and the east bank township of Torquay.

Devonport is also the terminus for the Bass Strait ferry Abel Tasman and as such is the starting point for many tourists.

The first settlement near Burnie was at Emu Bay in 1829 but the main town is now situated further west along the coast.

Burnie is the commercial centre of the region with several large industries and an outlet for the surrounding primary industries with rail heads and ports.

Further along the coast is the fascinating township of Stanley below the spectacular Nut mountain.

Stanley is almost a town time has forgotten with original cottages and fishing as the major source of income.

A former Prime Minister of Australia, the late Joseph Lyons, was born at Stanley and his cottage is well marked.

The discovery of alluvial gold led miners to the West Coast settlement of Queenstown which supported 14 hotels at one stage.

Strahan is the major port of the West Coast and it still retains the flavour of the copper boom.

Strahan is also the starting point for the famous Gordon River cruise and a view of Settlement Island, the State's first penal prison, and the setting for Marcus Clark's novel For the Term of His Natural Life.

Although the level of mining on the West Coast is decreasing, the stark mountains of Queenstown and museums in Zeehan and Strahan have created a new gold mine for visitors.

The Abel Tasman ferry on her arrival in Tasmanian waters on 20th June, 1985.
She is the new flagship of Tasmania's tourism services across Bass Strait.
The Abel Tasman was bought from West Germany for $26 million.

The ANL Empress of Australia leaves Devonport on one of its last trips across Bass Strait to Melbourne. The Empress was replaced in 1985.

An aerial view of Burnie from 2000m – Table Cape is in the background.

An aerial view of Ulverstone, midway between Devonport and Penguin, taken from 2000m.
Devonport is in the background.

Above: Planting swedes at Bruce Cutts'
farm near Devonport. From left:
Sonia Sheridan, Rodney Brett, Irene
Sheridan, Dianne Brett and Bill Brett.

Left: The Nut with the township of
Stanley below.

114

Top: Irrigating potatoes near Burnie. North-West Tasmania supports a huge vegetable industry.

Above: The spectacular view of oats being harvested at Ridgley, south of Burnie.

The old Bayview Hotel at Stanley which was originally licensed in 1842 as the Shamrock Inn. Pictured are Toby and Luke, Sue, Louise, Anne, Jon, Rocky the dog, Ricky, Julia and Therese.

*Top: Close friend John Lovell and daughter Karen pull their boat ashore at sunset at
Picnic Point, Smithton.*

Above: The popular tourist resort of Boat Harbour.

Top: *The small rural township of Mole Creek, near Deloraine, with the Western Tiers in the background.*

Above: *The rural valley of Gunns Plains, 23km south of Ulverstone.*

Opposite page: *The evening haze over farmland, just west of Sheffield with Mt. Roland in the background.*

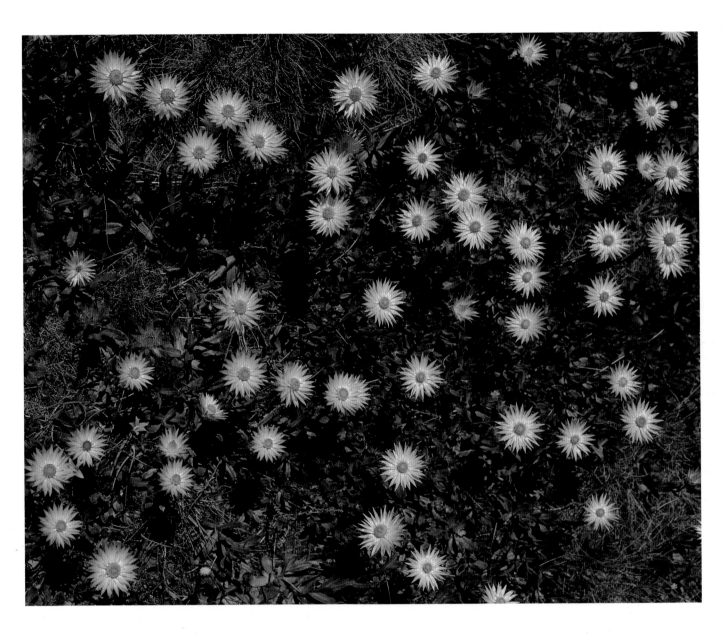

Yellow everlasting daisies, Hetichrysum acuminatum.

Previous page: The unsurpassed beauty of Cradle Mountain at sunrise with Dove Lake in the foreground.

*Right: The trigger plant,
Stylidium graminifolium.*

*Below: The Xyris often found in
swampy ground on the West
Coast.*

Barn Bluff (1559m) just south of Cradle Mountain. The swirling mist set alight by the rising sun gives fire and life to the mountain.

Frenchman's Cap Peak (1443m) where the headwaters of the Franklin River begin.

The Murchison Highway north of Rosebery. Mt. Murchison is in the background.

The historical West Coast mining town of Zeehan. The town was originally founded on silver and lead but is best known for the Renison Tin Mine at Renison Bell. The West Coast Pioneer's Museum has one of the best mineral collections in the world.

The unusual mineral-colored mountains beside the Lyell Highway near Queenstown. Mt. Owen is in the background.

Queenstown identities Aubrey Bennett, Merv Oxley (mine tour guide), Harry Jones (tour guide) and Frank Prowse.

The sleepy West Coast fishing town of Strahan on Macquarie Harbour. Strahan is the starting point for the spectacular Gordon River cruises.

Top: The Gordon River cruise ship James Kelly leaves Strahan.
Above: The Gordon River cruise boat Gordon Explorer takes many tourists on a memorable trip up this beautiful river.

An early morning aerial shot of the Gordon River as it snakes toward Macquarie Harbour.

Top: Sir John Franklin Falls where they enter the Gordon River at Warners Landing.
Above: A boat disappears into the mist on the Gordon River near Warners Landing.

Moss and fungi.

Evening light catches the top of gum trees in typical West Coast rain forest.

A Gordon River punt usually made of Huon Pine at Strahan.

Opposite page: Pink clouds settle over Ocean Beach at sunset near Strahan.

Mrs. Sue Cullen hanging out bull kelp to dry at Currie on King Island. The kelp is dried, milled and exported to Scotland.

Opposite page: The rugged coastline on King Island's west coast near Admiral Beach, just south of Currie.

INFORMATION SECTION

The Tasmanian Coat of Arms.

The Tasmanian Blue Gum Floral Emblem

HIRE CARS: This is the most popular form of travelling in Tasmania for tourists because the relatively short distances between towns and cities allows plenty of flexibility. Cars are available from all major centres but during summer forward booking is advisable.

DRIVING: If you hold a current driving licence in any Australian State or Territory you are permitted to drive in Tasmania for a period not exceeding one year on your current licence.

The Royal Automobile Club of Tasmania offers assistance to any motoring visitor who is a member of an automobile club or association in another State.

CAMPING and CARAVANS: This type of accommodation is very popular and well suited to Tasmania's spectacular sites and national parks. There are about 50 caravan parks in Tasmania and those registered with the Tourist Department have a grading. Specific rules apply to camping in National Parks and the respective rangers will provide that information and should be informed of your visit for safety reasons.

FISHING: This is an increasing attraction with many thousands of lakes and lagoons for trout fishing plus a rapidly growing game fishing industry off the East Coast. Charter boats are available from most ports with the best tuna fishing between May and July. Trout fishing requires licences which are available for three days, two weeks or a full season at varying rates.

TELEPHONE: Tasmania is divided into three area codes – 002 for the Hobart and southern area; 003 for Launceston and the North-East and 004 for the North-West and West Coast. Local information on telephone numbers can be obtained by ringing 013 and for other places in Australia and outside the local area code 0175. Enquiries are available 24 hours a day on 012. Fire, police or ambulance can be called on 000.

The Tasmanian flag was proclaimed on 25th September, 1876 by the Governor of Tasmania, Frederick Aloysius Weld.

SNOW SKIING: Tasmania is fortunate to have snowfields within about an hour's drive of Launceston and Hobart. Coaches serve both Ben Lomond which is 61km from Launceston and Mt. Field which is 96km from Hobart.

GOLF: There are about 60 courses ranging from championship level to neat nine hole layouts. Most are available to visitors on enquiry.

HORSE RACING: An active galloping and pacing program supports a healthy racing industry in Tasmania. Events are held weekly and mid-week in Hobart, Launceston and the North-West with many smaller country meetings.

TRANSPORT: Interstate travel is either by air or sea. The new Bass Strait ferry Abel Tasman, which offers an overnight service from Melbourne to Devonport is popular for visitors and should be booked well ahead during peak times.

CURRENCY: Australian dollars.

POPULATION: 432,000 (1983 census)

TOTAL STATE AREA (including islands) 68,331 sq. km.

Above: The Tasmanian Tiger which is thought to be extinct. Several intensive searches in recent years have failed to prove its existence despite reliable sightings. Preserved specimen photograph by Bob Green.

Below: A Tasmanian Devil photographed at the Rutherglen Holiday Village.

TASMANIA
HIGHWAY MAP SHOWING PRINCIPAL DISTANCES

KING
ISLAND
26 · Naracoopa
Currie
24 · Grassy

· Palana

45
FLINDERS

Whitemark ISLAND
24
· Lady Barron

CAPE BARREN IS.

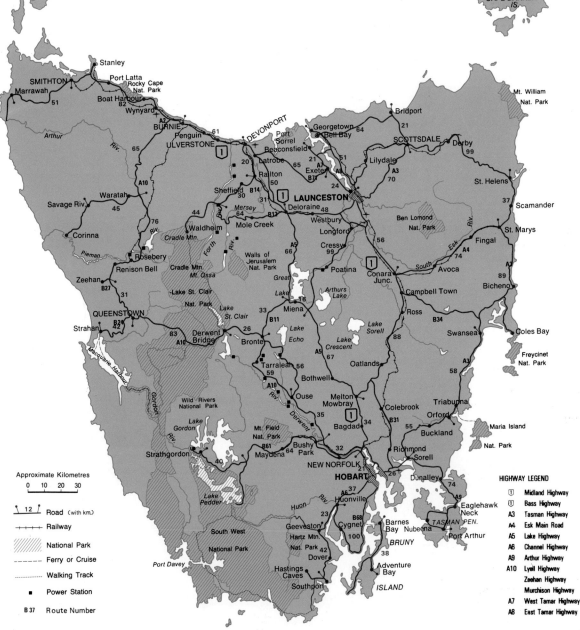

· Stanley
Port Latta
Rocky Cape Nat. Park
SMITHTON
Marrawah
Boat Harbour
51   82
Wynyard
A2
BURNIE   61   DEVONPORT
Penguin   Port Sorrel
ULVERSTONE   Beaconsfield
Arthur Riv.   65   20   Latrobe   65   A7   51
                            Railton   21   Exeter   A8
                            50   B71   24
A10   Railton   Georgetown · Bell Bay
Waratah   Sheffield   B14   LAUNCESTON
30   31   Deloraine   48
Savage Riv.   45   44   Mersey   Westbury   A3   70
        76   64   Mole Creek   Longford
Corinna   Waldheim   A5   Cressy   56
        Cradle Mtn.   Walls of Jerusalem   66   99
Rosebery   Cradle Mtn.   Nat. Park   Poatina   Conara Junc.
Renison Bell   Mt. Ossa   Great   Arthurs Lake   Campbell Town
Zeehan   Lake St. Clair   Lake   South   Ross
B27   31   Nat. Park   Lake St. Clair   Avoca   89
QUEENSTOWN   33   16   Miena   Lake Sorell   B34   Bicheno
B24   42   B11   Lake Echo   88   Swansea   Coles Bay
Strahan   83   Derwent Bridge   Lake Crescent   Freycinet Nat. Park
        A10   26   Bronte   A5   Oatlands
        Tarraleah   56   67   58
        59   Bothwell   A3
        A10   Ouse   Melton Mowbray   Triabunna
        35   34   Colebrook   Orford
Strathgordon   Lake Gordon   Bagdad   B31   55   Buckland   Maria Island Nat. Park
        B61   Mt. Field Nat. Park   32   Richmond
        40   Bushy Park   Sorell
Maydena   64   NEW NORFOLK   Dunalley   74
        HOBART   26   A9
Lake Pedder   A6   37   Eaglehawk Neck
        Huonville   TASMAN PEN.
South West   23   Barnes Bay · Nubeena
National Park   B68   Cygnet   Port Arthur
        Geeveston   100   BRUNY
        Hartz Mtn.   38
Port Davey   Nat. Park   42   Adventure Bay
        Dover   ISLAND
Hastings Caves
Southport

Mt. William Nat. Park
Bridport   21
SCOTTSDALE   Derby
        99
Lilydale   St. Helens
A3   37   Scamander
70   St. Marys
Ben Lomond Nat. Park   Esk Riv.   Fingal
        A4   74

Approximate Kilometres
0 10 20 30

⌐12⌐ Road (with km.)
+++ Railway
▨▨ National Park
- - - Ferry or Cruise
...... Walking Track
■ Power Station
B 37 Route Number

HIGHWAY LEGEND
①	Midland Highway
①	Bass Highway
A3	Tasman Highway
A4	Esk Main Road
A5	Lake Highway
A6	Channel Highway
A9	Arthur Highway
A10	Lyell Highway
	Zeehan Highway
	Murchison Highway
A7	West Tamar Highway
A8	East Tamar Highway

A Dedication to My Parents

My father John, known as Jack, was born in the original homestead on this little farm called Inglewood at Chain of Lagoons on the East Coast in 1898. My mother Elsie was born in Victoria in 1902 and settled with her parents at Piccaninny Point.

My father was of Welsh descent and my mother of English-Irish ancestry.

They were married at Piccaninny Point at 7.00 a.m. on 28th October, 1925. They lived and worked on the farm and had four children, Margery, Claire, Brian and myself.

My father was a quiet, gentle and hard working man with a deep affection for the farm on which he was born. He was very much the strong and silent type. He passed away on 9th October, 1979.

My mother was a forthright person but with a soft heart and an understanding of my love for photography.

She always encouraged me. She passed away on 7th March, 1984.

I still miss them both.

Owen Hughes